The Light o' Wales

Tony Denton and Nicholas Leach

▲ The lighthouse at the end of Holyhead Breakwater.

◄◄ (Front cover) The Skerries lighthouse off the coast of Anglesey.

◄ (Frontispiece) Bardsey lighthouse.

Published by
Landmark Publishing Ltd
The Oaks
Moor Farm Road West
Ashbourne
Derbyshire DE6 1HD
England
Tel (01335) 347349
Fax (01335) 347303
landmark@clara.net
www.landmarkpublishing.co.uk

British Library Cataloguing in Publication Data. A catalogue record for this book is available from the British Library.

ISBN 9781843064596

Layout and design by
Nicholas Leach
Printed by Cromwell
Press, Trowbridge

Contents

Welsh Lighthouse History

This book provides a comprehensive round-the-coast guide to the lighthouses and harbour lights on the coast of Wales, from south to north, starting with the lights in the Bristol Channel and going north and then west, ending at the Dee estuary. The Welsh lighthouses form a distinct and compact group which includes some notable architectural towers of historical significance.

While the Corporation of Trinity House is responsible for most of these lights, including all the major ones, many significant small harbour lights are also in operation, and details of these have been included. This introduction provides a general overview of lighthouse development and organisation in England and Wales, focusing on the need for lights to mark the Welsh coast, and looking at how Trinity House has developed into the service it is today.

The first lights

Trading by sea has been a principal activity of all civilisations, yet moving goods and cargoes by water involves facing difficulties and dangers such as storms and bad weather, avoiding reefs, headlands, sandbanks and cliffs, and making safe passage into ports and harbours. The need for aids to navigation is therefore as old as trading by sea itself and, today, modern lighthouses operated by Trinity House are supplemented by a plethora of small, locally-operated lights of varying sizes and range, mainly around ports, harbours and estuaries, to aid the safety of vessels.

The earliest aids to navigation were beacons or daymarks sited near harbours or ports rather than on headlands or reefs, to help ships reach their destinations safely. The earliest lighthouses were in the Mediterranean and the oldest such structure of which written records survive was that on the island of Pharos, off Alexandra on Egypt's north coast. The Pharos lighthouse, which stood 466ft tall, was built between 283BC and 247BC and lasted until 1326.

The exact site and date of the first navigational lights to be shown from a part of the modern Welsh coastline are not known, although a Roman date has been suggested for possible lighthouse towers at both Flint and Holyhead. However, without firm evidence of any Roman building, it is probable that a medieval lighthouse at St Ann's Head was the oldest such structure in Wales. The next oldest was that at The Skerries off the north-west tip of Anglesey, followed by Flatholm in the Bristol Channel.

The development of lighthouses around the coasts of the British Isles mirrored the development of trade routes. The earliest British lights were situated on the south and south-east coast of England in order to assist vessels trading with France and north European ports. By the seventeenth century, the emphasis had changed, with lights along the east coast

established to help colliers carrying coal from ports in the north-east to London.

The changes in port usage are reflected in the evolving pattern of lighthouse construction. The expansion of trade through Bristol, passing South Wales, was also significant and led to the building of the light on Flatholm. While Bristol declined, the great coal ports of South Wales expanded, and eventually the impressive natural harbour of Milford Haven became a major port in the area, along with smaller ones at Swansea, Cardiff, Newport and Barry, all requiring their own aids to navigation.

Colonial trade involving west coast ports expanded during the eighteenth and nineteenth centuries, and came to be dominated by Liverpool, although London remained the largest port. The port's expansion, which created the need for lighthouses, was considerable; between 1772 and 1805 inward shipping, largely from America and the West Indies and including cargoes such as tobacco and sugar, increased from 77,000 to 331,000 tons, while the ignominious slave trade also played a role in port expansion.

As Liverpool expanded, to manage and run the port's affairs, the Liverpool Harbour Authority was set up in 1762 which, with its successor the Mersey Docks and Harbour Board, was responsible for the establishment and maintenance of a number of significant lights on the approaches to the Mersey, many on the Welsh coast from Anglesey eastwards.

The dominance of the Liverpool trade alongside the Welsh coast is illustrated by the evidence of the lighthouse dues collected from ships passing Smalls lighthouse in

▲ The lighthouse built in 1829 on Caldey Island is still operational, although the attached cottages are now leased as holiday homes.

Pembrokeshire in 1831–32. From ships docking in Liverpool £11,206 was collected, while trade to Swansea, Neath, Bristol and Beaumaris was only worth £1,000 and £1,600 in dues for each port. Trade from Belfast, Dublin, Wexford, Cork, Glasgow, London and Hayle was worth between £100 and £1,000 in dues paid.

Trinity House

The organisation responsible for the operation and maintenance of the major aids to navigation today is the Corporation of Trinity House. The exact origins of Trinity House are obscure, but probably date back to the early thirteenth century when groups of tradesmen, such as seamen, masters of merchant vessels and pilots, formed guilds to protect their interests.

One of the earliest such organisations was the Deptford Trinity House, which was incorporated by Royal Charter after its members had petitioned Henry VIII to prohibit unqualified pilots on the Thames in 1513. Deptford was then a busy port and the main point of entry for the capital's trade, so pilotage duties were lucrative and Trinity House members wanted to retain their monopoly. Another similar organisation was the Trinity House at Newcastle-upon-Tyne, which was responsible for early aids to navigation on the Tyne at the time of its charter in 1536.

However, the Newcastle body's involvement in providing aids to navigation proved the exception rather than the rule as, despite erecting some towers in East Anglia, Trinity House was generally reluctant to build lighthouses. Instead it encouraged entrepreneurs to consider building them as profit-making undertakings. As a result, private lighthouse ownership became relatively widespread during the seventeenth century and the number of private lighthouses increased during the following centuries. Choosing the best position for a light, with sufficiently busy ports nearby

▼ The Point of Ayr lighthouse overlooking the Dee estuary as modified in 1820. Now disused, the tower remains but the attached building has been demolished.

The Pier Head, Cardiff

from where revenue could be collected, was crucial for the light to yield a good return.

Although a proliferation of unnecessary lights was prevented, private light owners gained a reputation for greed and lights were built around the coast on a somewhat haphazard basis. As a result, large areas of the coastline remained unlit, and by the nineteenth century, with the level of trade increasing as Britain's industry expanded, the situation was clearly unacceptable. Trinity House had to accept the new demands, with the leases expiring on many privately-owned lighthouses forcing the Corporation to take over. In 1807, Trinity House assumed responsibility for the Eddystone light off Plymouth, and the next three decades saw considerable changes to lighthouse organisation in England and Wales.

These changes were formalised in 1836 with an Act of Parliament giving Trinity House of Deptford Strond complete authority over lighthouses and making it the body to which others, including the regional Trinity House organisations, had to apply for sanction of the position and character of lights. Although by this time the majority of English lights were under the jurisdiction of Trinity House, the 1836 Act centralised lighthouse management.

The 1836 Act also gave the Corporation the power to use a compulsory purchase order on all privately-owned lights. Although only ten lighthouses were still in private ownership,

▲ A postcard from the early twentieth century showing a lighthouse at Alexandra Dock, Newport. Now demolished, this light was probably erected in 1875 when the dock was built but little more is known about this light.

the compensation paid to owners cost the Corporation a staggering £1,182,546. The most notorious of all the patents was that dated 13 July 1714, giving William Trench permission to build a lighthouse on the Skerries and to collect a compulsory levy from passing shipping for upkeep of the light. Skerries became the most profitable lighthouse around England and Wales and its owner in the nineteenth century, Morgan Jones II, refused to accept any offer until the matter was settled in court.

Between 1836 and 1841, he was offered £260,000, then £350,000 and finally £399,500 by Trinity House, but rejected each. However, he died in 1841 before the final negotiations were completed. A jury eventually awarded £444,984 in compensation in July 1841, thus demonstrating the considerable profits that were to be made from lighthouse ownership. Even after Trinity House took over The Skerries and halved its levy, the light still made a huge profit.

By the mid-nineteenth century more ships traded along the west coast and around Wales than anywhere else, and consequently the dues paid to the owners of The Skerries lighthouse and Smalls lighthouse were greater than those paid to any other in the UK. In 1852 £23,000 was paid for the use of Smalls light, about £18,000 for The Skerries, while other lighthouses in the British Isles raised about £5,000 or less in annual revenue. By 1822 the standard lighthouse due collected at British ports was one farthing per ton.

Once all the private lighthouses had been taken over, Trinity House gradually assumed control of lighthouse maintenance and construction during the nineteenth century. During the great period of lighthouse construction between 1870 and 1900, Victorian engineers and designers constructed and modernised at least fifty stations and built new rock towers. Lighthouses were also established at the major ports, and the major harbours of Holyhead and Fishguard, developed in the nineteenth and early twentieth centuries respectively, both had significant lighthouses built to help guide ships in and out of port.

Harbour lights

Much of the literature about lighthouses has concentrated on the major lights, which are often impressive structures in spectacular locations. However, no less important are the many smaller lights found at most ports and harbours. They have developed in response to specific local circumstances, so their design, construction and purpose differ markedly and the variety of such lights around England and Wales is considerable.

Many harbour authorities are responsible for their own aids to navigation, and this has led to a variety of lights and beacons

being erected. Some ports, where vessels need to follow channels, have leading or range lights which, when aligned, mark a safe passage. Others have long piers or breakwaters, the limits of which need marking, and on these some of the finest light towers have been constructed, such as that at Fishguard.

In areas like the north-east of England, where trade between ports was competitive, new harbours were built with grand lighthouses to mark their entrances, such as at Tynemouth and Whitby. In other areas, such as Wales where the main trade

▲ The light on the east bank of the river Usk is typical of the smaller lights that help guide ships into a specific port.

◀ The lighthouse at the end of Holyhead Breakwater when it was manned. Originally operated by Trinity House, it is now under the auspices of the port authority Stena Line.

▲ Situated on the cliff edge, Nash Point high light was operated in conjunction with a low light until the 1920s to mark the Nash Sands, and is one of the most impressive towers on the Welsh coast operated by Trinity House.

was in raw materials, more modest lights were erected at places such as Burry Port and Barry Dock. The growth of passenger vessels saw ports such as Fishguard and Holyhead vie for trade and build new harbours with lighthouses.

Lightkeepers

Throughout the history of lighthouses, the lightkeeper has played an essential role in maintaining the light and keeping the lighthouse in working order. However, during the latter half of the twentieth century, the era of manned lighthouses came to an end as automation took over. Before automation, however, every light

had to be manned.

The idealised view of lighthouse keepers conjures up a somewhat romantic image of men living in a tower with only the sea for company. While this was accurate for remote rock stations, such as Smalls, where keepers were confined to fairly cramped quarters for weeks at a time, the reality for most keepers was a little different. The lights on the mainland had a senior keeper who would be supported by two assistant keepers, usually with families. With automation, the lights are controlled from a central location with a locally-based attendant who is responsible for the general maintenance of the station.

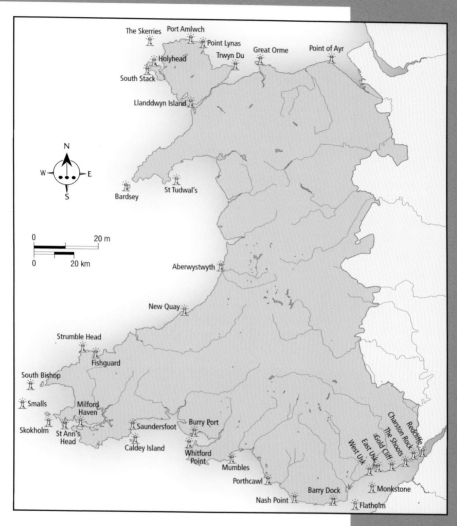

The lighthouse entries start on the south coast with the lights in the Bristol Channel on the Welsh side, and go west and then north to Anglesey, then east to the Dee estuary, ending at Point of Ayr. The photographs show the lighthouses as they are today, and a number of historic images have also been included. The information about visiting the lighthouses should be used only as a starting point, and it is advisable to consult road maps and Ordnance Survey maps if visiting any of the places.

Redcliffe

ESTABLISHED
1886

CURRENT TOWER
1910

OPERATOR
Gloucester Harbour
Trustees

ACCESS
By walking down a
long public footpath
from Mathern Church
across Caldicot Level

Situated on the shore about a mile north of Charston Rock, Redcliffe light was erected by the Great Western Railway Company in 1886, and in conjunction with the Charston Rock light formed a pair of leading lights through the Shoots, a narrow channel offshore. The fixed white light, powered by oil, was mounted on a wooden post.

The Gloucester Harbour Trustees, who took over responsibility for all aids to navigation previously owned and maintained by the Sharpness Lighthouse Trustees on 1 January 1891, commenced a programme of improvement and in 1910 they replaced the pole with a 33ft lattice steel tower. It was converted to acetylene gas with a flashing white light in 1926 and converted to electricity in 1965.

Following complaints that it was difficult to see, the white flashing light was changed to red for an experimental period in 1927, but was returned to white flashing and remained so until 1966 when it was changed to fixed blue. In 1982, when a back light was installed, the intensity of the light was increased by the installation of eight fluorescent tubes. A series of vertical white daymarks were also added to the mast.

The back light, situated 150 yards behind, consists of a 100ft abacus column with a bank of six blue fluorescent tubes. The Gloucester Harbour Trustees converted these and a number of other lights on the river to blue following complaints from local boat owners of background light pollution levels.

▼ This light was erected at Redcliffe in 1886 and is situated on the shore a mile north of Charston Rock.

Charston Rock

As vessels pass upstream along the river Severn towards Gloucester, they have to manoeuvre through a narrow channel offshore from Portskewett called the Shoots. To mark this channel, a pair of leading lights was erected by the Great Western Railway Company. The front light, although correctly called Charston Rock, is sometimes referred to by the name of the adjacent Black Rock.

Built in 1886, the 23ft white-painted stone tower had a vertical black line. Maintained by Sharpness Lighthouse Trustees, the oil-burning light was operated in conjunction with Redcliffe to show a channel through the Shoots.

On 1 January 1891 the Gloucester Harbour Trustees took over responsibility for all the aids to navigation previously owned and maintained by the Sharpness Lighthouse Trustees, including Charston Rock and Redcliffe. The Charston light was converted to acetylene in 1926 and, in 1966, to battery power using the lantern and lens from Redcliffe. The light showed an all-round beam with reinforcement on the leading edge. In 1980 the lantern was removed and replaced by an all-round lens powered by batteries and solar power.

Over time, a number of complaints were made about the light's visibility, and between 1927 and 1928 it was changed to red flashing. However, since then it has shown white flashing with the intensity increased to today's values, which give a five-mile range with a leading edge range of eight miles.

ESTABLISHED
1886

CURRENT TOWER
1886

OPERATOR
Gloucester Harbour Trustees

ACCESS
Best seen from the river, but it can also be viewed from the Black Rock picnic area east of Portskewett

▼ The light on Charston Rock, offshore from Portskewett, seen from Black Rock picnic area.

The Shoots

ESTABLISHED
1891

CURRENT TOWER
1986

OPERATOR
Gloucester Harbour
Trustees

ACCESS
Easiest by boat, but
distant views are
possible from the
west bank of the river
Severn to each side
of the Second Severn
Crossing road bridge

The Gloucester Harbour Trustees, being aware of the need for good marking of the navigable channel, looked at the Shoots and, although the channel was marked by the leading lights at Charston Rock and Redcliffe, thet erected two pole beacons in 1891 known as the Upper and Lower Shoots Beacons. One beacon was on the western extremity of the English Stones, and the other on the edge of the high rock north of Sand Bay.

In 1892, the Upper beacon was removed and relocated on the edge of the rock just above the Lake. These beacons were significant as they were the first aids to be erected by the Trustees outside their area of jurisdiction. In 1949 a report suggested the lighting of these two beacons, as the lower beacon was two miles south of Charston Rock light and a light would greatly aid those entering the channel. However, although a request for loan monies was made in 1951 nothing was forthcoming, so the plan did not go ahead. In 1965 a further request to light the beacons resulted in the improvements to Charston Rock and Redcliffe described earlier.

The decision in 1986 to build a second Severn road crossing meant that the Shoots channel would be even more hazardous as vessels would need to alter course to avoid the new bridge's supports. As a result, four 53ft reinforced concrete beacons were erected in addition to lights on the bridge. The beacons were formed from pre-cast concrete rings with a concrete platform. The lights were powered by mains, wind or solar and from north to south are:

Lady Bench: a red column supporting a solar powered quick flashing red light. This is the front light, with Lady Bench Rear mounted on a steel gantry on one of the road bridge supports.

Old Man's Head: a yellow column with a black band supporting a solar-powered very quick-flashing white light, giving nine flashes every ten seconds.

Mixoms: a red column supporting a solar-powered flashing red light, giving three flashes every ten seconds.

Lower Shoots: a yellow column with a black band supporting a solar-powered quick-flashing white light, giving nine flashes every fifteen seconds.

► The Lady Bench light seen from the picnic area at Black Rock, with the Lower Shoots beacon beyond the road bridge, a supporting column of which can be seen far right.

▲ This yellow column, situated on the east side of the channel to the north of the motorway bridge, is known as Old Man's Head.

◄ The most northerly light in The Shoots Channel, situated on the west side of the channel, is known as Lady Bench.

Gold Cliff

This unique light is situated on a grassy bank just south of the village of Goldcliff. Operated by the Newport Harbour Commissioners, it consists of a 9ft oblong sheet steel box with a pyramid roof. There is no lantern and the simple light is mounted on top in a circular lamp holder. Erected in 1924, the mains electricity operated white light had a range of six miles and, when active, the white light had a range of six miles.

Some indication of its age can be gauged by the fact that it was powered by mains electricity, but it has been redundant for several years judging by the condition of the steel. The light originally marked the most southerly part of the headland to the east of the river Usk, where a channel passes close inshore of the Welsh Grounds. The erection of the beacon on Denny Island probably influenced the decision to disconnect this light.

► The deteriorating light at Gold Cliff stands near the cliff edge on the most southerly point of the headland to the east of the river Usk.

Situated on the river bank east of the Usk, where the river joins the Bristol Channel, the East Usk lighthouse is operated by Newport Harbour Commissioners. It was erected in 1893 by the Commissioners and housed a second light at the mouth of the river to indicate the channel which, at that time, was close to the east shore. The light was operated in conjunction with the older light on the opposite bank at West Usk. The lighthouse on the east side of the river consists of a 36ft white prefabricated cylindrical steel tower mounted on six screw-pile legs.

The tower is topped by a gallery and a hooded lantern, which houses an electrically-powered flashing white light marking Sea Reach Channel with red and green sectors to either side. The light, visible for fifteen miles, is under the supervision of an attendant. The area around the tower is a nature reserve.

ESTABLISHED
1893

CURRENT TOWER
1893

OPERATOR
Newport Harbour Commissioners

ACCESS
Take the road from Newport to Uskmouth Power Station, park in the nature reserve car park; then a walk through the levels of the reserve and the lighthouse can be easily seen

◄ Situated on a nature reserve to the east of the river Usk, this light is the only operational one of what was originally a pair marking the entrance to the river.

West Usk

▶▶ In its current much altered state, the West Usk lighthouse has a replacement flat roof and a replica lantern.

Ships entering the port of Newport encounter a dangerous tidal race off St Brides where the rivers Usk and Severn meet, and this tidal race is the second fastest in the world. To guide vessels in the area, a patent for the construction of a light was first sought in 1807. This original application came to nothing, but in 1820 it was renewed and Trinity House subsequently commissioned a lighthouse on what was then an island on the west bank of the river Usk.

Correctly called West Usk lighthouse, it is also known as St Brides. The lighthouse, the first designed by James Walker, was a slightly tapered 56ft circular brick tower with gallery and lantern. Two lights, visible for eleven miles, were displayed from the lantern, one white and one red, with another white light 14ft lower down on the tower.

Some time before the end of the nineteenth century, keepers' dwellings were added in the form of a two-storey oval building surrounding the tower. This unusual structure is something of an architectural gem, particularly given the fact that it was James Walker's first lighthouse.

Although the brick buildings and tower were rendered and painted white, the lantern, complete with its conical roof, was painted black. The light was discontinued in 1922 and the lantern removed. The lighthouse was then cropped at gallery level and a shallow pitched roof added, while the cast iron gallery railings were retained.

Because of its location, the whole structure was mounted on a circular bed of solid granite blocks with a cast iron handrail. The handrail was cut off just above ground level after the light was decommissioned. In 1995, the present owner purchased the deteriorating building and restored it. The pitched roof was removed from the tower and a replica lantern installed with a cone-shaped roof, not dissimilar to the original, apart from the structure being painted white.

▶ (Left) An old photograph showing the West Usk lighthouse in its operational days.

▶ (Right) This bell currently hangs at the door to the West Usk lighthouse, which is now a bed and breakfast establishment.

WELCOME TO THE WEST USK LIGHTHOUSE BUILT 1821

Monkstone

ESTABLISHED
1839

CURRENT TOWER
1993

OPERATOR
Trinity House

ACCESS
Can only be reached
by boat

►► Monkstone
lighthouse at
high water.

▼ The Monkstone
lighthouse at low
tide, with its unique
fibreglass extension
standing on a rock
visible at low tide.

Three miles upriver from Flatholm is Monkstone rock, a submerged reef which only breaks the surface at low spring tides. Located about three miles east-north-east of Lavernock Point and five miles south of Cardiff near to Flatholm Island, it is one of many obstacles to shipping in the area. Other hazards include sandbanks which are passable only at high tide but exposed at low water.

The lighthouse on Monkstone therefore not only marks the rock but also forms a reference point for the other hazards. The original 45ft granite tower, built in 1839, was an unlit beacon. However, in 1925 it was strengthened and fitted with a circular cast iron tower complete with a gallery,

an iron lantern and an automatic acetylene light. The stone tower was reinforced with both horizontal and vertical iron bands which, along with the new tower and lantern, were painted red.

In 1993 it had a unique update when the iron tower and lantern were replaced by a red prefabricated 30ft cylindrical fibreglass unit. Mounted on top in polycarbonate lamp holders are main and auxiliary lights powered by solar panels mounted in a vertical formation on the circumference of the fibreglass tower. This increased the height of the lighthouse to 75ft and improved the range of the flashing white light, which gives one flash every five seconds, to thirteen miles.

Flatholm

ESTABLISHED
1737

CURRENT TOWER
1820

AUTOMATED
1988

OPERATOR
Trinity House

ACCESS
Visiting the island, an historical and nature reserve, is possible via boat trips from Barry Dock

▶▶ The impressive lighthouse at Flatholm dates from the eighteenth century.

▼ The island of Flatholm, dominated by the lighthouse, is the most southerly point of Wales.

The area of water known as the Mouth of the Severn lies partly in England and partly in Wales, with the ports of Avonmouth and Bristol on the English shore and Cardiff, Newport and Chepstow on the Welsh side. There are a number of aids to navigation on both shores, but for the purpose of this volume only those on the Welsh side will be described.

As ships travel upstream, the first hazard is the island of Flatholm, the most southerly point of Wales, which lies approximately three miles south-east of Lavernock Point in the centre of the shipping channels where the Bristol Channel meets the Severn Estuary. It is perhaps surprising therefore that considerable wrangling took place before a light was displayed there. As early as 1733, John Elbridge, a member of the Society of Merchant Venturers of Bristol, petitioned for a light but to no avail.

In 1735, William Crispe informed Trinity House, he had taken a lease on the island and wished to build a light in their name but at his expense. He did of course wish to recoup his costs from ship dues. This again was rejected, but, after sixty soldiers were drowned in a wreck near Flatholm in late 1736, a further proposal by William Crispe was accepted and a 70ft stone tower was built on the summit.

Its coal light was first displayed on 1 December 1737. The elevation of the coal burner was such that it was the greatest in Wales, with only Flamborough Head in England exceeding it. Unfortunately for Crispe and his partner, they went bankrupt and handed the lease to Caleb Dickensen. In 1790 a severe lightning storm damaged the lighthouse and for a time the light had to be displayed from ground level.

Following complaints about the inadequacy of the light, Trinity House took over the lease in 1819. By 1820 they had increased the height of the white stone tower to 90ft and installed a lantern and an oil-fired Argand lamp with reflectors which

Flatholm

▶ Line drawings showing the successive adaptation of the lighthouse at Flatholm. The original eighteenth century structure has survived, with the walls almost 7ft thick at the base. The rebuilding of 1867 increased the height of the tower to almost 100ft.

1737   1820   1867

displayed a fixed white light. In 1825, the height of the light was increased by a further 5ft and a fountain oil lamp installed.

Further alterations were made in 1866 at which time a new iron gallery was fitted to the top of the stone tower and a larger lantern with a more powerful optic was installed. This increased the height of the lighthouse to 99ft. The light characteristic was altered to occulting in 1881. A Douglas multi-wick burner was installed in 1904 to improve matters, and

in 1923 this was superseded by a Hood paraffin burner.

Equipment rooms were attached to the tower and the keepers' families were housed in cottages next to the lighthouse. In 1929 the lighthouse was redesignated a rock station and the families were withdrawn. The keepers left in 1988 when the station was automated, and in 1997, the lighthouse was converted to solar power. The flashing white light is visible for fifteen miles, with a red sector visible for twelve.

Barry Dock

In the nineteenth century the South Wales coal trade had expanded to such an extent, and the Taff Vale railway and Cardiff docks were so congested that they virtually ground to a halt. As a result, in the 1880s a new port was opened at Barry Dock.

As part of this development, a stone breakwater was built out from Barry Island, and in 1890 a 30ft white circular iron tower with gallery and lantern, complete with cupola roof and weather vane, was built on the end by Chance Brothers to a standard design. Painted white with a red lantern roof, it shows an electric quick-flashing white light visible for ten miles.

ESTABLISHED
1890

CURRENT TOWER
1890

OPERATOR
Associated British Ports

ACCESS
Breakwater closed to the public, but local anglers fish from the end; access to the dock is via a long flight of steps from the main road above

◄ The small lighthouse on the end of the Barry Dock West Breakwater is fenced off by palisade fencing topped with razor wire to prevent vandalism.

Nash Point

►► Nash Point Low Light and the adjacent keepers' cottages have been converted into holiday homes

▼ The Low Light when in service, with the High Light under construction.

The entry to the Bristol Channel is impeded by a series of sandbanks known as Nash Sands, where the channel begins to narrow at the headlands between Porthcawl and Barry and making navigation for shipping more hazardous. In February 1830 an application to build an aid to navigation to mark the area was made by Thomas Protheroe, of Newport, together with a number of other owners from the Bristol area and, as a result, they established a pair of range lights at Nash Point about three miles east of St Donats in 1832. Designed by James Walker, they were built by Joseph Nelson, who died a year after their completion.

The High Light, situated to the east, is a 122ft cylindrical stone tower complete with gallery and lantern. Initially it was painted with broad black and white horizontal bands, but it was repainted white when the Low Light was disconnected. In 1851, manning levels at Nash were increased and the attached keepers' dwellings added.

In conjunction with the Low Light, it showed a fixed white light over the safe passage with a red light over the sands. When it became the sole light, the light configuration was amended to occulting white visible for sixteen miles with a red sector visible for ten miles. The lantern was glazed with rectangular panes but in 1867 it was replaced by a delicately glazed helical lantern as seen today.

The Low Light was situated about 300 yards to the west, and consisted of a white-painted 67ft conical tower complete with lantern and gallery similar to the high light. Unlike the High Light, the attached keepers' dwellings were erected in 1832 when the light was commissioned. Its light

Nash Point

▶▶ Nash Point High Light was the last operational lighthouse in Wales to be automated, and regular tours of the lighthouse are carried out most weekends.

▼ The imposing fog horn, on the roof of the compressor house, is often activated during visitor tours.

characteristics were identical to the High Light, as were the optics. It was discontinued in the 1920s when the High Light was reconfigured. By the 1970s, the lantern had been removed.

The original lights consisted of double rows of reflectors with thirteen Argand burners in the high light and twelve in the low light. When the high light was electrified in 1968 the Argand burners were replaced by a rotating optic. Today a 1,500-Watt lamp and a first order catadiotric fixed lens with two reinforcing panels gives a group flashing light twice every fifteen seconds with ranges of white, twenty-one and red sixteen miles.

Nash Point was the last South Wales lighthouse to be demanned with the light

automated in 1998 and the keepers withdrawn two years later. For a while during the automation programme the station controlled Mumbles and Flatholm lighthouses as well as Breaksea Light Float.

The 1903-built Ruston Hornsby 20hp generator and fog signal compressor from the station were acquired by Leicester Industrial Museum in 1966. The modern foghorn is mounted on top of a white square flat-roofed engine room to the seaward side of the road, half way between the high and low lights and is sounded during the weekend visitor tours. In 1977, after the tuberous thistle was found on the site, the area inside the compound was designated a Site of Special Scientific Interest.

Porthcawl

►► The small
lighthouse at the
end of Porthcawl
breakwater.

▼ Heavy seas crash
on the breakwater.

Although the harbour at Porthcawl was established in 1825 to service the metal trade, it was not until 1860 that a lighthouse, called Porthcawl Breakwater Light, was erected on the end of the stone breakwater. Although appearing ordinary at first glance, it is in fact one of only two surviving cast iron lighthouses in Wales. It consists of a 30ft hexagonal tapered tower without a gallery. Access to the light is via a cast iron doorway and an internal ladder.

When first commissioned, the light shone through a plain opening and the top had a pitched roof. It was painted to imitate a stone structure. The light was replaced in 1911 by the current arrangement; the top was removed and a replacement round-domed lantern with a Chance Brothers optic was crudely attached to the top of the tower.

The light, visible for six miles, is displayed through a glazed window and shows a fixed white light over the channel with red and green sectors to the sides. It was coal- and then gas-fired and, in 1974, it was converted to mains gas. It was eventually electrified in 1997, making it one of the last in Wales to be so converted. The tower is currently painted white with a broad black band at the base.

Swansea

ESTABLISHED
1792

CURRENT TOWER
1909 and 1971

OPERATOR
Trinity House

ACCESS
The lights are part
of the dock complex
which is difficult to
access, although they
can be seen from the
outside of the marina

Although no lighthouses can be seen at Swansea today, a number of interesting lights have been built here. In 1792, when the west pier was to be built, a lamp was erected on a post at its proposed termination. In 1803, with the pier complete, a 20ft cast-iron octagonal tower was erected on the end. Designed by William Jernegan and cast at Neath Abbey, it stood on a stone plinth and had a small octagonal lantern. It was lit by candles in 1810, then by oil in 1845. Maintained by Swansea Harbour Commissioners, it was moved to the end of the pier when the pier was extended in 1878.

In 1909 the pier was again extended and the light replaced by a cast iron lantern with a domed top mounted on a wooden platform supported by a wooden trellis. In 1971, the east pier was reconstructed in reinforced concrete and a light, called Swansea East Pier, consisting of a concrete post with a simple light, was erected on the end. Showing a flashing red light, it is visible for nine miles.

In the early nineteenth century a 20ft white tower was built on the end of the inner east pier. In 1909 it was replaced when the pier was extended and a light, which still exists, was erected on the end of this structure. This consists of a 23ft wooden framework supporting a simple lantern showing a fixed green light, which is visible for seven miles. These lights are within the dock complex and are difficult to approach.

The first-order Fresnel lens, which was installed at Mumbles Head lighthouse, was given to the Swansea Transport and Industrial Museum in 1987. It is not on display but kept in storage at the museum. Between 2002 and 2005 the museum was rebuilt as the National Waterfront Museum.

▶ On display as a floating exhibit at the National Waterfront Museum is the old Helwick Lightship No.91, 104ft in length and built in 1937 by Philip & Son, Dartmouth. It has a hexagonal tower complete with lantern and gallery.

To guide ships past the Mixon Sands and Cherry Stone Rock, where hundreds of ships have been lost, Swansea Harbour Trustees were given a licence to erect a lighthouse on the outer of the two outcrops at Mumbles Head in the late eighteenth century. Work started in 1792 but in October that year the partly-constructed lighthouse collapsed.

Plans for a new light by William Jernegan, a local architect who had also been responsible for the Swansea light, were drawn up and in 1794 Trinity House gave the harbour trustees a ninety-nine-year lease on the lighthouse, which was completed later that year. In addition to the tower, a pair of two-storey keepers' houses was built. Two coal-fired lights were proposed, one above the other, to be distinguishable from the

two lights at St Ann's Head and the single light at Flatholm. Thus came about the peculiar shape of the 56ft white stone octagonal tower, which is stepped halfway up, with a gallery at each stage.

Keeping two coal fires lit was expensive and so in 1799 a single oil light, with Argand lamps and reflectors in a cast iron lantern above the higher of the two galleries, was fitted. By the Act of 1836, the light was taken over by Trinity House which had further improvements carried out in 1860, when a dioptric light was fitted. The lens was configured in such a way that there appeared to be two beams of light, which partly simulated the original configuration.

In 1905 the characteristic was converted to an occulting light, and to produce the flashing light a hand crank was used to wind

ESTABLISHED
1794

CURRENT TOWER
1794

AUTOMATED
1934

OPERATOR
Trinity House

ACCESS
At low water, it is possible to walk from the beach by the pier across to the island, but the rocky terrain is not easily crossed; best viewed from the pier or the car park on the headland with vantage points along the adjacent coastline

▼ Mumbles lighthouse is surrounded by the remains of the Palmerston's fort.

Mumbles

▶▶ The Mumbles lighthouse is accessible at low tide but, as can be seen from this photograph, it is only possible to reach it with great care and no little effort.

a series of weights. These were attached to a lever mechanism that raised and lowered a metal cylinder around the light, but within the Fresnel lens, thus making the light appear to flash. The periods of dark and light could be adjusted to give different light characteristics.

Further changes were made in 1934, when, on the retirement of the last keeper, the station was modernised and the optic replaced. In 1969 an overhead electricity line was erected from the mainland and the light converted to electrical operation. By 1977 the original cast iron lantern had deteriorated and was removed. It was superseded in 1987 when the lantern and light from Lightvessel No.25 was transferred to Mumbles. The original first-order Fresnel lens was donated to the Swansea Transport and Industrial Museum for display.

In 1995 the station was converted to solar power and the main and emergency lights replaced by a pair of biformed Tideland M300 lanterns powered

by quartz halogen lamps, one housed in the lantern room and another above. The group flashing white light is visible for sixteen miles. At the same time, fog detector equipment was installed; the fog signal, with a range of two miles, gives three blasts every sixty seconds. Control of the lighthouse, which was the last coal-fired tower to be built in Britain, was the responsibility of the British Transport Docks Board until Trinity House took over in 1975.

Between 1859 and 1861, one of Palmerston's forts was built around the tower but it was never used for its original purpose. It was, however, used to accommodate a small battery of soldiers during the Second World War before being decommissioned in 1957. Today, solar panels for the light are fixed to the top of its remains. Also on the island are the ruins of gun emplacements, while little remains of the original keepers' dwellings which were built onto the rock to the landward side of the lighthouse tower.

▶ This historic photograph shows the now demolished keepers' dwellings at Mumbles lighthouse. The original cast iron lantern was also in place at this time.

Whitford Point

In the nineteenth century, Llanelli was an important port and many ships entering the Loughor Estuary were lost off Whitford Point and its extensive sandbanks. As a consequence, Captain Luckraft, the Llanelli harbour master, designed a wooden lighthouse to be positioned about half a mile north of Whitford Point. Sometimes known as Chwittfford but more correctly as Whitford Point, it was erected in 1854 but so severely damaged by storms the following year that it had to be abandoned. After being repaired in 1857, it was later struck by the vessel Stark and extensively damaged.

By 1864 the lighthouse was such a problem that the local commissioners agreed to plans by John Bowen, a local engineer, for a new lighthouse 300 yards to the south. Built by Bennet & Co, it was first lit in November 1866 and consisted of a 44ft ornate tapered cast iron tower with a gallery and lantern. Its flashing white light was converted to automatic gas operation by the Llanelli Harbour Trust in 1919, after which it was visible for seven miles. In 1921 the Trust built a new lighthouse to the south at Burry Holms, and the Whitford Point Light was extinguished in 1926. The Burry Holms light was itself discontinued in 1939.

During its operational life, the lighthouse's cast iron panels kept loosening. Bands were placed around the tower from 1880 onwards and by 1885 it was reported that 150 had been fastened round the cracking plates. The foundation on soft sand also gave concern, and concrete and stones were placed around the base in 1886. Despite these problems and seventy years of disuse, this, the only offshore cast iron lighthouse in Britain, still exists, having been a listed monument since 1979.

In 2000 the Llanelli Coastal Millennium Park attempted to save it from crumbling into the sea by offering it for sale at £1 on the proviso that the new owner repaired it. It was thought an agreement had been reached but this fell through and the lighthouse is still available to anyone willing to part with at least £100,000.

►► The historic cast iron lighthouse at Whitford Point at high tide is surrounded by water. However, it can be approached at low tide by a long walk across Whitford Burrows and then with care across the beach.

► The lighthouse at Whitford Point is fully exposed at low tide.

Burry Port

▼ Situated on the
Western Breakwater
at Burry Port, this
lighthouse was fully
restored in 1996
by Llanelli Borough
Training.

The harbour at Burry Port was built between 1830 and 1836 to replace that at Pembrey, 400 yards to the west. In its heyday, Burry Port was the main coal-exporting port for the valleys, but now the dock houses the only marina in Cardiganshire, for which extensive dredging was carried out in 2005.

In 1842, Trinity House gave permission for the Burry Port Harbour Authority and Navigation Commissioners to erect and maintain a lighthouse on the end of the west breakwater of the outer harbour. As this was a harbour light, the annual cost of its upkeep, which amounted to £32 in 1844, was not met by dues on shipping.

Sometimes known as Burry Inlet but more correctly Burry Port, the light consisted of a 24ft white-painted stone tower with a black gallery and red lantern. In 1995–6 the tower was restored by Llanelli Borough Training with the support of the nearby Burry Port Yacht Club, and a light, donated by Trinity House, was installed.

The restored light was formally opened on 9 February 1996 by the Mayor of Llanelli, Councillor David T. James. The current white flashing light is visible for fifteen miles. The light is now a significant landmark for the users of the nearby marina.

The neighbouring port of Pembrey Old Harbour also had a small lighthouse at one time to guide shipping into that port, but neither the light nor the port remain in existence.

The small picturesque harbour at Saundersfoot was built in the 1840s to export coal and lime from the surrounding area. In 1848 the Saundersfoot Harbour Commissioners erected an 11ft circular rubblestone lighthouse, with a door on its north side, on the end of the south harbour wall. Initially lit by candles, the light was housed in a peculiar lantern made up of iron glazing bars with an arched stone top bolted to the top of the tower.

An interesting feature was the use of a tide gauge, which consisted of a float in the harbour connected by wire to a red glass which obscured the light when there was insufficient water to enter. The light was converted to oil in 1861, as candles were considered inadequate.

The light was discontinued in 1947 following the closure of the local mines, but was relit in 1954. The old lantern was removed, the top of the lighthouse was rebuilt in rubblestone and a polycarbonate holder showing a flashing red light visible for seven miles was displayed.

ESTABLISHED
1848

CURRENT TOWER
1954

OPERATOR
Saundersfoot Harbour Commissioners

ACCESS
The pier is open to the public

◄ The small light on Saundersfoot South Pier was discontinued in 1947 but rebuilt and re-commissioned in 1954 when the port was revived as a yachting harbour used predominantly by pleasure craft. With the light holder added to the roof, the height of the structure increased to 17ft.

Caldey Island

►► The lighthouse on Caldey, which marks shoals and sands, is on the island's southern shore at the highest point.

▼ The lighthouse and its associated buildings from the landward side.

Although the lighthouse on Caldey Island is in a prominent situation on the highest point, it is the monastery that attracts most visitors. Monks first came to Caldey in the sixth century and, in the twelfth century, Benedictines from nearby St Dogmaels set up a priory on the island and remained until the Dissolution of 1536. In 1906 pioneering Anglican Benedictines purchased Caldey and built the present abbey, but their stay was relatively short, as financial difficulties forced them to sell in 1925; the present monks are of the Cistercian order.

The lighthouse, sometimes called by its Welsh name Ynys Byr, operates in conjunction with Lundy North and guides ships past St Gowan Shoals to the south-west and Helwick Sands to the south-east. Designed by Joseph Nelson and built by Trinity House in 1829 at a cost of £4,460, it consists of a 52ft circular white-painted tower with lantern and gallery. The original light consisted of twenty Argand lamps and reflectors.

A single-storey service building at its base is attached to a pair of two-storey keepers' dwellings. The light, which stands 64ft above high water, was initially oil-powered, but was automated and converted to acetylene in 1927 at which point the keepers were withdrawn and the cottages sold. The lantern itself was installed around the middle of the nineteenth century.

Caldey was the last Trinity House light to be operated by acetylene gas. A part-time keeper was employed to maintain the light until 1997 when the lighthouse was modernised and the light source changed to mains electricity. The new light is a 500 Watt halogen lamp with a second order 700mm catadioptric optic giving a flashing white light visible for thirteen miles. The light has two flashing red sectors which are visible for nine miles.

Milford Haven

ESTABLISHED
1870

CURRENT TOWER
1870 and 1970

OPERATOR
Milford Haven
Conservancy Board

ACCESS
West Blockhouse
and Watwick are
approached via Dale
then the road to St
Ann's Head; turn left
into Maryborough
Farm road, then right
to both locations; East
and West Castle Head
are approached via
the Pembrokeshire
Coast Path from St
Ishmael's; turn left
into Sandy Haven
onto a single track
road past Skerryford,
then a gated path
to both lights; other
lights are best
viewed from the
Haven as they are in
industrial areas

▶▶ The beacons
at West Blockhouse
Point at the entrance
to Milford Haven,
situated about a
mile north-east of St
Ann's Head.

▶ The range lights
at West Blockhouse
Point with (just
visible on the cliff
edge below the
fort) the red beacon
erected by Trinity
House in 1957.

Vessels entering Milford Haven pass St Ann's Head lighthouse and then turn into the haven itself. To mark the West Channel a pair of leading lights designed by James Douglass was erected in 1870 by Trinity House on the north shore at West Great Castle Hill Head, four miles west of Milford Haven town. These lights were eventually handed over to Milford Haven Conservancy Board who operate them today.

The Front Range is a 17ft high square stone tower without a lantern situated on the cliff edge. There are dwellings at the rear. Painted white, the tower has a vertical black stripe and the buildings are trimmed with a black cornice. Of the two lights, one is shown through a narrow window and the other is a sector light on the roof. One is fixed red, white or green dependant on direction, with the other a flashing white light. Since 1970, when the lights in the area were modified, these lights have been sealed beam units visible for fourteen miles mounted on the roof alongside a radar antenna.

The Rear Range, 170 yards behind the Front Range on the ramparts of the old Iron Age fort, was a 42ft square tower of similar design without a lantern. The flashing white light, visible for sixteen miles, was shown through a narrow window, but was discontinued in 1970 when new aids to navigation were erected in the area. One of the improvements was the erection of a new light at East Little Castle Head. This new Rear Range replaced the old West Great Castle Head Rear Range light, and works in conjunction with the Front Range to mark the safe channel between St Ann's Head and the Mid Channel Rock.

The light was designed by Posford Pavy and is three-quarters of a mile from the original one. It is a curved circular 85ft white tower with a board containing a vertical black band and two lines of solar panels near the top. The sealed beam light units, which are mounted on a gallery on top of the tower, give an occulting white light visible for fifteen miles. So as not to obscure the new Rear Range, the height of the old Rear Range tower was reduced to 21ft.

Further improvements by Posford Pavy involved the

Milford Haven

erection of four reinforced concrete towers on the east side of St Ann's Head, three at West Blockhouse Point and one at Watwick Point. The West Block House structures consist of three octagonal reinforced-concrete towers 30ft, 37ft and 46ft in height, topped by octagonal concrete platforms supporting sealed beam lights.

The two outer columns carry black square daymarks and their flashing white lights operate as a pair of leading lights. The centre light has an octagonal black and white daymark and its flashing white light, visible for thirteen miles, operates as a Front Range to the Watwick Point light marking Haven Approach.

Situated about half a mile to the north at Watwick Point is the Rear Range which consists of a curved circular pinkish white tower similar to East Castle Head, but taller at 160ft. A large board contains a vertical black and white daymark near the top. The mains-powered sealed beam light units mounted on a gallery on top of the tower give a flashing white light which is visible for fifteen miles.

In 1957 Trinity House erected a beacon on the steep cliffs below West Blockhouse Fort. This consists of a round red metal lantern mounted on a concrete base located on the sheer rock face and reached by a steep flight of steps from the fort. The light was obtained second-hand from Rame Head lighthouse.

The whole of the Haven is extensively marked with aids to navigation, most mounted on the oil jetties. Two sets of leading lights are of note. On the south shore at Popton Point, opposite Milford Haven, are two Front Range lights mounted on steel lattice towers on the jetty, one outboard with a white diamond daymark and the other inboard with a white circular daymark. These operate with a Rear Range at Bullwell to mark the extremities of the channel to the south of Stack Rock. The Bullwell light is on a lattice tower carrying an arrowhead black and white daymark on the headland.

Further up the Haven, on the north side at Newton Noyes, is a similar formation of two Front and a common Rear Range to mark the Milford Shelf between the oil terminals. In the grounds of the oil depot on steel lattice towers, the inboard Front Range has a diamond black and white daymark and the Outboard Front Range and Rear Range both have a black and white daymark. All show fixed red lights. In the channel south of St Ann's Head is a rocky outcrop which is marked by a 40ft circular steel pole light called Mid Channel Rock.

►► This graceful structure at Little Castle Head is of similar design to, but at 85ft somewhat shorter than, the 160ft tower at Watwick Point.

▼ The lights on the building at Great Castle Head now form a Front Rrange with Little Castle Head.

St Ann's Head

St Ann's Head is the oldest lighthouse on the Welsh coast and stands on the western side of the entrance to Milford Haven, one of Britain's finest deep water harbours and used by tankers. The approach to the port can be hazardous, with dangerous reefs, situated almost mid-channel and in two groups, having to be negotiated. One of the greatest dangers, seven miles south-east of St Ann's Head, is the Crow Rock and Toes off Linney Head, a reef which has claimed many vessels. In addition to providing guidance for vessels using the Haven, the lighthouse is an important mark for passing coastal traffic, warning of the offshore dangers.

The first attempts to provide a light for the area were made in 1662, when Trinity House approved in principle a coal-fired light at St Ann's Head, supported by voluntary payment of dues, to guide Milford-bound shipping. However, the owners extracted dues illegally from shipowners and the light, then the only one on the west coast, was ordered to be extinguished by Parliament in 1668, a somewhat extreme measure given the lack of any other lights on the coast. Drawings suggest that this tower formed the western tower of a destroyed chapel, which is said to have commemorated the landing of Henry Tudor in the Haven in 1485 to claim the English throne.

Forty years passed before another light was established, although the local merchants petitioned many times for lights to be provided throughout the period. However, not until 15 March 1713 was a patent granted to Trinity House to build a lighthouse at St Ann's Head. Following its policy of the time, Trinity House leased the patent to the owner of the land, Joseph Allen, for ninety-nine years at an annual rent of £10. Allen agreed to build two lighthouses and keep them in good repair. To fund the lights, he was permitted to collect dues from the shipmasters at Milford Haven amounting to one penny per ton of cargo on British vessels and two pence on foreign vessels.

▶▶ The original high light had its lantern removed and an observation gallery was added. The bulk of the building is now painted black and the accommodation is available as holiday rentals.

▶ The original high light, seen when in operaton, was discontinued in 1910 but remains standing.

St Ann's Head

Allen established two towers near the old disued lighthouse, and coal fires were lit on them for the first time on 24 June 1714, before the lease was actually signed, highlighting the urgency of the matter. The use of two lights was to distinguish St Ann's from the single light at St Agnes in the Isles of Scilly. The High Light was a 75ft white-painted tapered masonry tower with a single-storey keepers' building attached, and the light was visible for twenty miles. In 1800 Trinity House installed reflected Argand lamps in lanterns, which cost £600 and was paid for out of the light dues. The Brethren also managed the lights at a charge of £140 per annum.

The front or lower light was rebuilt in 1841, when cliff erosion endangered the old tower. The new 42ft octagonal masonry tower with lantern and gallery, attached to a two-storey keepers' house, was situated 30ft from the cliff edge and this serves as the present lighthouse. When the rear light was discontinued in 1910, a Matthews burner was installed in the front light, and in 1958 the station was converted to mains electricity with generators for stand-by. The lantern in the discontinued light was removed early in the Second World War and the room was converted into an observation room.

The automation of the lighthouse was completed on 17 June 1998 when the keepers were withdrawn. The white and red light flashes every five seconds, with the white light having a range of eighteen nautical miles and the red seventeen. An area control station between 1983 and 1998, St Ann's was manned by four keepers and supported helicopter operations to Smalls, Skokholm and South Bishop after automation. Although unmanned, the lighthouse remains an operating base for Trinity House's maintenance teams.

▶▶ The lighthouse at St Ann's Head has been automatic since 1998.

▼ The lighthouse guards the entrance to Milford Haven. The adjacent keepers' buildings, pictured on the left, are not occupied.

Skokholm

The small island of Skokholm, which is just over a mile long and half a mile wide, lies off the Pembrokeshire coast. The island's high cliffs rise sheer from the sea to well over 100ft in places and it is a renowned seabird sanctuary. The lighthouse, situated on its south-west point, makes up the landward corner of a triangle of lights with South Bishop and Smalls, guiding ships clear of a treacherous coastline into Milford Haven or up the Bristol Channel.

The station was built during the First World War to the design of Sir Thomas Matthews and was first lit in 1916. The lighthouse buildings are unique in being the last built by Trinity House using traditional building materials. The white-painted brick hexagonal masonry tower, 58ft in height, complete with gallery and lantern, is unusual in that it is built into the two-storey keepers' buildings in the centre of the front elevation with a slight vertical projection in the front wall above a square front porch.

Before the lighthouse could be built, a jetty had to be constructed on the island so that building materials could be landed. Subsequently, the jetty was used for landing stores and supplies, which were taken the mile to the lighthouse on two small trucks running on a narrow gauge railway. The trucks were originally pulled by a donkey, which was subsequently replaced by a tractor. When the station was manned, relief was by tender from Holyhead, but now it is reached by helicopter.

Although records show it was first lit in 1916, a plaque inside the building says that it was officially opened in 1915. In the early 1970s a new electrically-powered Chance fourth order catadioptric rotating optic was installed and the lighthouse was automated in 1983. The light, visible for twenty miles, flashes every ten seconds, white or red, and is solar powered. The fog signal engine room is situated on the seaward side of the building.

▶▶ Skokholm lighthouse from the air. The buildings are constructed of stone rubble which is rendered and painted white. The solar panels on the roof of the service buildings can be clearly seen.

▶ The lighthouse is more than 175ft above high water and the tower itself is 58ft tall.

Smalls

ESTABLISHED
1776

CURRENT TOWER
1861

AUTOMATED
1987

OPERATOR
Trinity House

ACCESS
Can only be seen by
boat or helicopter

Smalls is one of Trinity House's more remote offshore lighthouses and has an unusual and intriguing history. The small rock on which the lighthouse stands, situated about twenty-one miles west of St David's Head, is one of two tiny clusters of rocks lying close together in the Irish Sea, the highest of which projects only 12ft above the highest tides.

For more than two centuries a lighthouse on Smalls has warned passing ships of the rocks' dangers, with the first lighthouse erected there in 1776. The plans for this lighthouse were made by Welshman John Phillips, an assistant dock manager at Liverpool. He advertised for a tower design and selected that proposed by Henry Whiteside, a musical instrument maker from Liverpool who, in 1772, designed a model for the Skerries tower.

Whiteside's design for Smalls consisted of an octagonal timber house or hut perched atop nine legs or pillars, five of wood and three of cast iron, spaced around a central timber post, allowing the seas to pass beneath. The structure was 66ft tall and 17ft in diameter. The keepers' accommodation was at the top, just below the lantern. Welsh miners were employed to dig the foundations and undertake much of the construction work,

▶▶ The present Smalls lighthouse was completed in 1861 and was painted with broad red and white bands to distinguish it from other similar towers. These lasted until June 1997 when they were sand blasted off.

▶ An accurate drawing, by Douglas Hague, of Henry Whiteside's lighthouse of the eighteenth century after a number of extra oak struts had been added to strengthen the original nine.

Smalls

although progress was slow because of bad weather during winter 1775–6. While postholes were being dug at the rock, the tower was built at Solva, a small harbour on the mainland. In spring 1776 the whole structure was taken to the rock for assembly.

By September 1776 the oil lamps were lit, but Whiteside's tower was not strong enough to cope with the conditions on the rock and it had to be abandoned in January 1778 after a series of storms. Repairs were too costly and difficult to carry out, particularly as Phillips had no funds, and so he withdrew the keepers and extinguished the light. He handed over his interest to a group of Liverpool merchants who persuaded Trinity House to take over the tower.

The Brethren obtained an Act of Parliament in 1778 which authorised the repair and maintenance of the light and the collection and levying of dues. Phillips was then granted a lease on 3 June 1778 for ninety-nine years at a rent of £5. The tower was reinforced and relit in September 1778 and remained

▶ The elegant nineteenth century circular stone lighthouse on the Smalls, with the solar panels mounted near the lantern added since automation in the 1986. The light remains one of the most important aids to navigation for shipping in the area.

in operation until 1861, when it was replaced. It suffered considerable damage a number of times and as a result had to be strengthened. Trinity House eventually bought the lease in 1836 for £170,468.

The light is supposedly the scene of a tragic episode which occurred around 1800 and involved two lighthouse keepers, Howell and Griffith. Apparently, Howell died unexpectedly one night and Griffith put the body in a coffin which he made from the interior woodwork and lashed to the lantern rail outside. When the usual relief boat arrived, having been prevented by storms from getting close to the rock for several months, Griffith had been driven mad. After this, three keepers were always appointed to lighthouse teams.

The present lighthouse, 141ft tall, was built under the supervision of Trinity House's then Chief Engineer, James Douglass, to a Walker design based on Smeaton's Eddystone tower. The tower took just two years to build, a considerable feat, and was completed in 1861. It was painted red and white, but in June 1997 the stripes were no longer considered necessary and so the tower was grit blasted back to natural granite.

Various improvements were made during the 1960s and a concrete helipad was built over the station's water and oil tanks. This was replaced in 1978 by a helipad above the lantern, and automation came in 1987. The white light, which flashes three times every fifteen seconds, is visible for twenty-five miles.

▲ The lighthouse on Smalls seen on a rough day, with waves washing the rocks. An elevated helipad was constructed above the lantern in 1978 and the lantern itself was painted red during 1997.

South Bishop

▶▶ South Bishop lighthouse stands on the route of migrating birds which, attracted by the light's rays, flew into the lantern's glass panels. Many were killed and so Trinity House, in conjunction with the Royal Society for the Protection of Birds, built special bird perches on the lantern for use during the migration season and the mortality rate has been much reduced.

▶ South Bishop seen from the sea. Before helicopters, keepers had to climb steps cut into the sheer rock face to reach the lighthouse.

The rocky outcrop of South Bishop, also known as Emsger, is situated in St George's Channel, almost five miles south-west of St David's Head. The lighthouse operates mainly as a waymark for vessels navigating offshore and marks the northern entrance to St Bride's Bay. It also acts as a guide for vessels navigating around the Bishops and Clerks group of rocks, of which South Bishop is the largest and most southerly.

The lighthouse dates from the 1830s. An unsuccessful application for a light at South Bishop was first made to Trinity House in 1831 on behalf of shipping interests trading to Cardigan. Another application was made in 1834 on behalf of those using Bristol and St George's Channel, but a further five years passed before a light was constructed. Designed by James Walker and erected by Trinity House, the 36ft white-painted brick tower was completed and first lit in 1839.

The lighthouse tower has a lantern and gallery and is attached by a short corridor to a pair of two-storey pitched-roofed keepers' houses, which were intended for two families. However, due to the dangers of what is an extreme environment, it is doubtful if anyone other than the keepers lived on the rock, which is so exposed that the seas sometimes flood the courtyard and break lower windows. In 1971 a helipad was constructed on the island, but the pad was very exposed and often flooded in high tides and heavy seas, and so landing was not always practicable. Before helicopter, the keepers and their supplies were landed by tender.

The light was converted to electric operation in 1959, and automated and demanned in 1983. Since then, it has been converted to solar power with the solar panels situated between the lighthouse and the helipad. The current light, powered by a 70 Watt Mbi lamp with a fourth order catadioptric lens, flashes white every five seconds and has a range of nineteen miles. The fog signal is in an adjacent building and gives three blasts every forty-five seconds.

Strumble Head

ESTABLISHED
1908

CURRENT TOWER
1908

AUTOMATED
1980

OPERATOR
Trinity House

ACCESS
The island itself is not open, but an approach to the footbridge can be made from the Pembrokeshire Coast Path; it is possible to approach by car from Goodwick, near Fishguard, and the headland is signed along the minor roads

▶▶ Strumble Head lighthouse is siuated on a small island.

▼ The light covers the shipping channel out of Fishguard.

With the completion in 1905 of the new north breakwater at Fishguard, Trinity House looked at the aids to navigation required to safeguard shipping entering and leaving Cardigan Bay, particularly as steamers to Ireland were on the increase after the harbour opened in 1906 and Rosslare Harbour was developed on the Irish side of the Channel. They chose to build a lighthouse on the rocky outcrop called Ynys Meicl, or St Michael's Island, situated off the headland of Strumble Head. Completed in 1908, the light was designed to work in conjunction with South Bishop five miles off St David's Head in St George's Channel.

A narrow footbridge was built to connect the island to the mainland but even then the rocky outcrop made the building of the lighthouse as difficult as it would have been for a true offshore station. In order to get equipment across the gap and to the top of the outcrop, the builders constructed a jackstay cable between two winches, one on the headland and one adjacent to the lighthouse. This method is no longer used and all of the associated equipment has been dismantled and removed. Heavy items are now brought to the station by helicopter. Another unusual feature is that one handrail on the bridge doubled as a pipe carrying oil into the tower's basement.

The lighthouse consists of a 56ft white circular stone tower complete with gallery and lantern. A pair of white stone flat-roofed keepers' dwellings is attached to the tower on the seaward side. To one side is a white single-storey flat-roofed service building built in 1967 to house a foghorn which replaced an earlier explosive fog signal.

Strumble Head

►► Close-up view of Strumble Head lighthouse tower which is 56ft tall and 148ft above high water. The first order catadioptric optic has a range of twenty-six miles and is the original one dating from 1908.

The charges for this signal were kept in a wood-lined white stone service building which can still be seen. It was originally classified as a rock station.

The original light source was paraffin, with a large mechanically-driven revolving lens system weighing four and a half tons and supported on a bed of mercury, showing a white flashing light. A massive clockwork mechanism rotated it, driven by a quarter-ton

weight which, suspended on a cable, dropped gradually down a cylinder running from top to bottom through the tower. The drive had to be rewound every twelve hours.

The light was converted to electricity in 1965, and the first order catadioptric unit produces a flashing white light visible for twenty-six miles. The light was fully automated in 1980 and is now controlled from the Control Centre at Harwich.

► The lighthouse and its associated buildings are maintained by an attendant who visits occasionally to make sure everything is in working order.

► The small island on which the lighthouse is situated is connected to the mainland by a bridge. The red handrail, to the right, carried oil at one time.

60

Fishguard

ESTABLISHED
1913

CURRENT TOWER
1913

OPERATOR
Stena Line

ACCESS
North breakwater
is only accessible
from ferry port by
agreement with Stena
Line; access to the
east breakwater is
on the roundabout
at Parrog adjacent
to ferry terminal
entrance; the range
lights are a climb from
the ferry terminal, and
the fog signal at Pen
Anglas Point is found
by a detour from the
coast path

▶▶ The lighthouse,
which is operated
by Stena Line, is
situated at the end
of the breakwater
and was completed
in about 1913 when
the breakwater itself
was finished.

▶ (Left) The lights
above the harbour
are fixed green
range lights visible
for five miles.

▶ (Right) The
light on the east
breakwater has
solar panels
mounted on each
side of the light.

In the early years of the
twentieth century a plan was
formulated to construct a harbour
at Fishguard which would rival
those at Southampton and
Liverpool and accommodate
ocean-going liners. In 1905,
the Great Western Railway
constructed not only a railway
terminal at Goodwick, just to the
west of Fishguard, but also an
800-yard-long stone breakwater
out from Pen Cw, or the Cow and
Calf, to enclose a huge area of
water to the north-west of the
old harbour at Lower Fishguard.

A year later, on 30 August
1906, the first ferry to Rosslare
set sail from the harbour and
in 1909 the liner Mauritania
stopped on her voyage from
Liverpool to New York. She was
unable to dock due to lack of
water depth but passengers were
ferried off by boat and a carnival
procession took place in the
town. Although the ferry trade
continued, that was the last the
port saw of the big liners.

When the northern
breakwater was built, a
substantial lighthouse was
constructed on the end. It
consisted of an octagonal 46ft
stone tower with a double gallery
and single lantern. The tower
was reduced in width at each
gallery. The area below the lower
gallery remains its natural stone
colour but the area above and
the domed lantern are painted
white. For such a fine lighthouse,
surprisingly little is known about
its history and today its flashing
green light, visible for thirteen
miles, is powered by electricity
with solar panels nearby. The
lighthouse also carries a fog bell.

The east breakwater itself was
built about 1913 and it is likely
that the light on the end is of the
same date. This light consists of
a 36ft open lattice steel tower
which supports a small solar-
powered red flashing light visible
for ten miles. On the hillside
above the ferry terminal is a pair
of white triangular range marks,
each of which has a small fixed
green range. These range lights
originally marked an Admiralty
mooring buoy to the north-east
of the northern breakwater
light, but this was removed in
about 1990. An electric-powered
compressed air foghorn is sited
approximately a mile to the
north-west at Pen Anglas Point.

New Quay

ESTABLISHED
1839

CURRENT TOWER
Not in existence

OPERATOR
Harbour Trustees

ACCESS
The site is open to
public and is on the
end of the pier

▼ The tower
which supported
a small directional
navigation light but
is now disused.

In the eighteenth and nineteenth centuries the resort of New Quay in Cardiganshire, not to be confused with Newquay in Cornwall, was a bustling fishing port. In order to improve the anchorage, several proposals were put to the harbour authorities for a larger pier or breakwater. In 1820 the engineer John Rennie proposed a breakwater and pier to enclose a large area of sea, but his scheme proved too expensive. Instead, a smaller breakwater, completed in 1835, was commissioned from Daniel Beynon.

In 1839, a 30ft tapered circular tower, operated by the Harbour Trustees and made of rough stone, was erected on the end. The white-painted tower did not have a lantern as such and the fixed white light visible for six miles was displayed through a window in the red domed top. In 1859 a violent storm swept away the end of the pier as well as its lighthouse. They were rebuilt and the light continued to shine until 28 February 1937, when it was again washed away.

With trade in decline and the harbour silting up, it was decided not to rebuild the light, known locally as the Pepper Pot. It has since been replaced by a polycarbonate navigation light on a wooden post, which carries a plaque as a memorial to those lost in the two World Wars. In 2006 the possibility of restoring the Pepper Pot was discussed. The pier is open to the public.

Aberystwyth harbour is fed by the rivers Ystwyth and Rheidol, the steepest river in Britain. In its heyday it was one of the busiest ports in Wales, with ships sailing regularly from there to Liverpool carrying grain, cheese, salmon, wine, whisky, and fruit. Today, however, its main activity is pleasure craft and in 1995 a new £9 million marina, named Y Lanfa, was opened for business and significantly remodelled the harbour by providing permanent berths for over 100 vessels.

To help guide these vessels into the tidal entrance, a small polycarbonate lamp holder showing a green light on top of a 30ft tower was built. The tower, situated near the end of the south breakwater, is painted white with two green bands and is formed from nine precast concrete rings.

ESTABLISHED
1990s

CURRENT TOWER
1990s

OPERATOR
Associated British Ports

ACCESS
On end of south breakwater which is open to public

◄ The green and white tower on the south breakwater at the entrance to Aberystwyth harbour.

65

St Tudwal's

▶▶ Only the light
tower at St Tudwal's
remains in Trinity
House ownership.

▼ Close-up of the
tower showing the
solar panels.

St Tudwal's lighthouse is situated on St Tudwal's Island West, one of two small islands in Tremadoc Bay on the southern side of the Lleyn Peninsula. According to tradition, the island is named after the saint who lived there in the sixth century, and the remains of a priory known to have existed in the eleventh century are to be found on the east of the island. The light was established to assist the schooners that carried general cargo and slate from the quarries of North Wales at a time when such trade was commonplace. It was needed because Bardsey light to the west was obscured from some directions to ships traversing the west side of Tremadoc Bay.

The site for the lighthouse was purchased by Trinity House in 1876 for £111. A 36ft cylindrical masonry tower, with lantern, gallery and adjacent single-storey keepers' dwellings, was completed the following year to the design of James Nicholas Douglass. The occulting white light was significant in that it was controlled by the first occulting optic apparatus manufactured by Chance Bros. The light is also notable for its conversion to acetylene operation in 1922 and its subsequent operation by means of a sun valve.

This mechanism, invented by the Swedish lighthouse engineer Gustaf Dalen, consisted of an arrangement of reflective gold-plated copper bars supporting a suspended black rod. When lit by the sun during hours of daylight, the black rod absorbed the direct heat which reflected from the other bars and expanded downwards, thereby cutting off the supply of gas. This innovation enabled the light to become unmanned and in 1935 the keepers' dwellings were sold. As with other Trinity House lighthouses, St Tudwal's is maintained by an attendant.

In 1995 the lighthouse was modernised, electrified and converted to solar-powered operation after which the light was powered by a 100-Watt halogen lamp and a second order 700Mm fixed optic with a red sector. The light displays one white flash with a range of fourteen miles and one red flash which has a range of ten miles every fifteen seconds.

Bardsey

ESTABLISHED
1821

CURRENT TOWER
1821

AUTOMATED
1987

OPERATOR
Trinity House

ACCESS
Bardsey is accessible
by passenger ferry
from Porth Meudwy;
the light at Pen Diban
can be reached by
walking from the ferry
landing site

▶▶ The distinctive
square tower
and fog signal on
Bardsey Island.

▼ The dwellings are
no longer occupied
and an attendant
maintains the site.

The small island of Bardsey, separated from the mainland by Bardsey Sound, was a place of ancient pilgrimage known as 'the island of 20,000 saints', with a journey there regarded as the equivalent of one to Rome. However, the Welsh name for the island, Ynys Enlli, means 'island of the tides'. As it is situated at the end of the Lleyn Peninsula, opposing currents can create boiling seas in the Sound with the often dangerous combination of wind over tide making navigation hazardous.

The two-mile-long island, home to colonies of sea birds and grey seals and part of a national nature reserve, is surrounded by outcrops of sharp rocks. The lighthouse, on the southerly tip where the land is flat, guides vessels through St George's Channel and the Irish Sea. The 99ft tower and single-storey keepers' houses were erected by Trinity House under the supervision of Joseph Nelson in 1821. The tower cost £5,470 12s 6d, with a further £2,950 16s 7d for the lantern which, in 1910, was raised to increase its range. Following this change, the Cardigan Bay lightvessel to the south was removed. The lighthouse tower, unusual in being square, is striped in red and white bands. The white light has a range of twenty-six miles.

In 1965 the lighthouse was electrified; in 1987 it was converted to automatic operation, and until 1995 was monitored from the Trinity House Area Control Station at Holyhead, but it is now monitored from Harwich. A locally-based part-time attendant carries out routine maintenance.

Llanddwyn Island

ESTABLISHED
1845

CURRENT LIGHT ESTABLISHED
1975

AUTOMATED
1987

OPERATOR
Trinity House

ACCESS
Within the Llanddwyn Island National Nature Reserve; the nearby pilot house contains a small display of local history

►► The 1845 tower on Llanddwyn Island displayed a light until 1975.

▼ The small tower which supports a small directional navigation light.

Llanddwyn Island is more of a peninsula than an island, except at the highest tides. It is situated on the south shore of Anglesey, about three miles west of the southern entrance to Menai Strait. The earlier history of the light on the southern tip of the island is uncertain but by 1823 two towers existed, presumably day marks.

The first accurate information is that in 1845 alterations were made to one tower, known as Twr Mawr, costing £250 7s 6d, and a light was first exhibited from there on 1 January 1846.

The white-painted circular 36ft tower has a conical slate roof with living quarters within the tower, similar to some local windmills. It was unique in that it displayed a light from a lamp room attached to the tower at ground level, with the tower itself used solely for accommodation.

The optic, which dates from 1861, consisted of a silver-plated reflector and Fresnel lens, and was originally lit by six Argand lamps with reflectors. The light, which was visible for seven miles, was made redundant in 1975 when it was transferred to a nearby tower. The lower half of the tower was painted red in 2004 for the film Half Light.

On the extreme seaward perimeter of the island, south-east of the 1845 light, is a white-painted conical tower, known as Twr Bach, which was built between 1800 and 1818 of rubble stone and has a domed top. A solar-powered electrical navigation light, operated by Trinity House, was placed on the top in 1975 to replace the light on Twr Mawr. The flashing light shows white or red depending on the direction, visible for seven miles and five miles respectively.

South Stack

▶▶ Looking down on South Stack lighthouse, a scene which has inspired visitors, artists and photographers. The lamp is 212ft above high water.

▶ An old postcard of South Stack shows that it has changed little. The picturesque scene has always been a favourite subject of postcard publishers and this one shows the steamer St Seiriol passing on her way to Holyhead harbour.

The tiny islet of South Stack Rock is separated from Holy Island, on the north-west coast of Anglesey, by 100ft of chaotic seas, and forms a significant danger to shipping entering or leaving Holyhead harbour. A lighthouse to mark the rock was first proposed in 1665, when a petition for a patent to erect a light was presented to Charles II. However, this was not granted and the idea lay dormant until the shipping lanes off Anglesey, on the approach to the port of Liverpool, became busier.

Almost 150 years later, in August 1808, the foundation stone was laid and on 9 February 1809, the lighthouse, built at a cost of £11,828, first showed a light. The station was designed by the engineer Daniel Alexander and built by Joseph Nelson. The 92ft white-painted stone tower, with single-storey keepers' quarters and a service building attached, was originally fitted with Argand oil lamps and reflectors and a revolving Argand lamp was installed in 1818.

Around 1840, a railway was constructed and this enabled a lantern, which displayed a subsidiary light, to be lowered down the cliff to sea level when fog obscured the main light. In the mid-1870s the lantern and lighting apparatus were replaced by a new lantern, and in 1909 an early form of incandescent light was installed. In 1927 this was replaced by a more modern type of incandescent mantle burner.

The station was electrified in 1938 and automated on 12 September 1984, when the keepers were withdrawn. The current first order catadioptric optic flashes white every ten seconds and the light has a range of twenty nautical miles.

The site has an unusual inverted fog bell, which weighs two and a half tons, and an ingenious arrangement whereby, when fog or low cloud obscured the light, a small clockwork-operated lantern, 10ft square and mounted on wheels, was lowered down a quarry-like railed incline to within 50ft of sea

South Stack

► An aerial view of South Stack shows the path down to the island, the keepers' accommodation and the fog horn.

►► South Stack lighthouse and fog horn from the sea. The horn gives a one second blast every thirty seconds and has a range of three nautical miles.

▼ South Stack lighthouse seen from the adjacent cliffs.

level. The builder and engineer of this unusual object was Hugh Evans. Only the bed of the incline survives. A compressed-air horn was later fitted on the site and this in turn has been replaced by an electronic fog signal.

Various methods of crossing the chasm between the mainland and the rock have been employed, starting with a hempen cable along which a sliding basket, carrying a person or stores, was drawn. This was replaced in 1828 by an iron suspension bridge, and then in 1964 by an aluminium bridge.

The present footbridge, completed in mid-1997, was funded largely by the Welsh Development Agency allowing the island and lighthouse to be reopened to visitors after thirteen years. The station is a Trinity House Visitor Centre, the only one in Wales, offering public access to the tower. The former Trinity House Fog Signal Station at North Stack was also sold off and is now owned privately.

Holyhead Admiralty Pier

► The lighthouse on Admiralty Pier seen from Irish Ferries fast craft Jonathan Swift.

▼ Admiralty Pier is in the old part of Holyhead harbour, with the tower significant because of the lantern's age.

Until the early 1800s, vessels at Holyhead moored in the creek beyond Salt Island and although a lighthouse was built to guide them, little is known about it. By 1821 work had commenced on what is now the inner harbour, while the Admiralty or Mail Pier was built out from Salt Island to provide berthing for the cross-Channel ships from Ireland. In the same year, John Rennie (1761-1821) had an earlier lighthouse, by Daniel, replaced by the one that stands today on the end of the pier. He also designed a similar lighthouse on the pier at Howth, the mail terminal for Dublin, and oversaw its construction.

The Holyhead light consisted of a 48ft tapered stone tower with a gallery and lantern. The iron railings around the gallery were ornate and the lantern, with a copper domed roof, was made up of four tiers of lightly-glazed panels. A wooden jetty was built around the lighthouse in 1864 on which a railway station was built.

When the outer harbour was completed in 1873, this light, often referred to as Holyhead Mail Pier Light or Salt Island Light, was subsidiary to the new breakwater light and was reduced to a signal light. Originally showing a white light visible for a mile, it later showed a red light.

At one time, two signal lights mounted on a pole were displayed above the lantern and these showed a white light when the inner harbour was open and a red light when it was closed. These lights have been removed, and the lantern light now shows lights in the configuration once shown on the pole. Around the tower the pier is now a workshop area for the port, while the tower itself is historically significant because of its designer.

Holyhead Breakwater

ESTABLISHED
1873

CURRENT TOWER
1873

AUTOMATED
1961

OPERATOR
Stena Line

ACCESS
The breakwater is accessible in good weather

▶▶ The lighthouse at the end of Holyhead Breakwater has a circular lantern with the domed apex surmounted by a weathervane.

▼ Holyhead Breakwater is the longest such structure in the country.

Holyhead port, which now caters mostly for ferry traffic to Ireland, was developed in the nineteenth century. Building the huge breakwater, which, at 1.87 miles long, is the UK's longest such structure, took twenty-eight years. Work began in 1845 and lasted until 1873, with an average of 1,300 men employed on the project. About seven million tons of limestone from Anglesey's eastern coast around Moelfre were used. The breakwater was officially opened on 19 August 1873 by Albert Edward, Prince of Wales.

Situated at the north-western end of the town, the breakwater was topped by a promenade leading from Soldier's Point and culminating in an impressive lighthouse, which was probably designed by John Hawkshaw, the superintendent engineer who oversaw the harbour works

from 1857 to 1873. The tower has a roll-moulded string-course projecting above the first floor level, and is unusual in being 22ft 3in square. Painted white with a single black horizontal band, it was completed in 1873 as work on the breakwater was coming to an end. A moulded cornice supports a walkway around the circular lantern.

The lighthouse was manned until November 1961 and was built square to make the living quarters more comfortable. One of the last keepers was David John Williams, who subsequently became a Trinity House speaker giving talks on the service. The tower is 63ft high and 70ft above the high water mark. The light has a range of fourteen miles and is the responsibility of the port authority, now Stena Line. Inside, much of the original living accommodation remains intact.

The Skerries

▶▶ The historic Skerris lighthouse, with the 1903 red sector light tower visible in front of the main tower.

▼ An old postcard of Skerries lighthouse before the red sector marker was built.

The Skerries are a small group of rocky islets, seven miles off Holyhead, to the north-west of Anglesey, which have some of the oldest lighthouse buildings in existence. The keepers' dwellings are reputed to be the oldest such buildings surviving in the British Isles. The treacherous nature of the waters and the amount of passing vessels made this rocky outcrop a magnet for speculators who saw that profits could be made from a lighthouse.

In 1658 a proposal was made for a light by the first of these speculators who wanted to profit from ships' dues. This, and another in 1705, were refused, but in 1713 a sixty-year lease was agreed, and in 1717 the first light, erected on the highest point of the island, was completed by the builder William Trench. It was coal-fired and despite predictions, it was not a financial success;

the owner died in 1725 in severe debt. To add to his woes he also lost his son off the rocks.

An Act of Parliament of 1730 enabled his son-in-law Sutton Morgan to increase the shipping dues and confirmed the patent on his heirs forever. In 1759 Trench's tower was rebuilt in limestone by Sutton Morgan's heirs at a cost of £3,000. The light, mounted on a slightly tapering 28ft tower, was displayed in a coal brazier. This tower was increased in height in 1804 by owner Morgan Jones, who had inherited it in 1778, and an iron balcony was added with railings enclosing the oil-burning lantern. The oil-burner was enclosed in a glazed lantern room and covered by a cupola.

In 1838 Trinity House began purchasing private lighthouses, but the owner of the Skerries refused to sell as his light had proved to be very profitable.

The Skerries

By 1840 it was the only private light left in England, but in 1841, after the death of the owner, the Corporation purchased it. Trinity House then had the station remodelled, and, in 1848, it was extensively altered by James Walker. A free-standing keepers' house was built, enclosed by a castellated-walled cobbled courtyard with private facilities, which still stand.

The tower was increased in diameter at its base with Walker's trademark design producing a reduction in its diameter halfway up. The balcony was rebuilt in castellated stone supported by brackets on corbels. A new cast iron lantern, almost 14ft in diameter with glazed square panes around a dioptric light with mirrors, was installed, topped by a finial. The light was then displayed from a height of 119ft above high water.

In 1903 a solid circular tower was added to the south-west of the tower to carry a sector light. Access to this tower is provided by an improvised landing in the main tower. The buildings for the fog signal, which gives two blasts every twenty seconds, are arranged concentrically around the main tower.

In 1927 the light was converted to electricity with the original generator later augmented by solar power. The 76ft tower, which stands atop the outcrop, is painted white with a broad red band, as is the adjoining engine room. The lighthouse was automated in 1987 and a helicopter pad was built nearby. Today the flashing white light, produced by a one kilowatt lamp and a first order catadioptric lens, gives two flashes every ten seconds and is visible for twenty-two miles.

▶▶ The solar panels can be seen to the front of the tower, with the stairway up from the landing stage.

▼ The treacherous Skerries rocks present a severe hazard to passing vessels.

Port Amlwch

▶▶ The 1853-built
building on the end
of the 1816-built
pier was at one time
a watchtower, and
until about 1972
also served as a
lighthouse.

▼ The 'old world'
charm of the original
dock remains
despite the erection
of a new concrete
dock to seaward.

Port Amlwch with its small harbour was once one of the busiest ports in Wales. Its expansion began in 1768, when the Parys Mountain copper mine, at that time the largest in the world, was opened and the harbour was enclosed by two small piers. At the end of each pier a small stone octagonal tower was built, displaying a white light from the top.

With increasing trade, there was a need to give extra protection to the harbour, so in 1816 a new 150ft-long outer pier was constructed. On the end of the new outer pier a 16ft square stone tower, with a white light visible for four miles, was commissioned in the same year. The New Seaman's Guide of 1821 stated that there were 'small white houses displaying lights at night', which would suggest that the light on the original short pier was still operational.

The new lighthouse, also used as a watchtower, was altered in 1835, and in 1853 the tower which exists today was built on the western end. This tower is not instantly recognisable as it consists of a 15ft slightly tapered tower with a rendered-brick lantern room roofed in local slate. The light, which was displayed through a window only visible from the seaward side, had a range of six miles.

It would appear that by this time only one light was displayed at the port. It is not certain when this light was declared non-operational but it was probably when a new fixed navigation light mounted on a white metal column was placed on the new dock, about 100 yards to seaward, constructed in 1972 for the Liverpool Pilots when their pilot boats and workshops moved to Amlwch from Point Lynas. The new concrete dock facility has not impinged on the old dock, which retains much of its 'old world' charm. In the churchyard of nearby St Elaeths Church is a lighthouse memorial gravestone.

Point Lynas

ESTABLISHED
1779

CURRENT TOWER
1835

AUTOMATED
1989

OPERATOR
Trinity House

ACCESS
Access to the inside of the complex is restricted, but the lamp room can be seen from the coast path

▶▶ The castellated square tower fronted by a ground floor lantern is sited on ground almost 40m above sea level.

▼ The castellated building at Point Lynas was designed by Jess Hartley, engineer to the Mersey Docks and Harbour Board.

Point Lynas, on Anglesey's eastern coast, was an ideal site from where pilots could board ships into or out of Liverpool. In 1779 Liverpool Town Council set up a pilot station and leased a house on the point from which, in order to assist shipping, two lights were shown out of windows in a building on a site about 300m to the south of the present site. Two eleven-inch reflectors provided small lights which were displayed to the east and west.

In 1781, the first part of the current castellated complex was built, primarily to provide accommodation for the pilots. It was also clear that the lights were inadequate as they were often obscured by smoke from the nearby industries and, more importantly, did not provide a light to the north-east quarter.

Although Alan Stevenson suggested that a 70ft lighthouse should be built to overcome the difficulties, it was decided to abandon the original location and move to a site up the hill to the north. In 1835, a two-storey extension was built onto the north side of the pilot station, including a ground floor 12ft semi-circular lamp room. This lamp room was increased in size to 15ft in 1874 and completely refurbished in 1879.

The original argon-powered light, visible for sixteen miles, was converted to oil in 1901. In 1951 generators were installed and the lamp was converted to electricity. Mains electricity was connected in 1957 and the occulting light, visible for twenty miles, was uprated.

During the refurbishment of the site in 1879, the local signal station was moved into the complex and a set of signal lights was displayed from a 75ft pole. This site, operated by the Mersey Docks & Harbour Co, was taken over by Trinity House in 1973; the light was automated in 1989, and the pilots moved to Amlwch Pier.

Trwyn Du

▶▶ Trwyn Du
lighthouse was built
in 1838, and its
stepped base made
it the first wave
washed light built by
James Walker.

▼ A small reef
between Puffin
Island and Penmon,
called Perch Rock,
is also marked by
this cone-shaped
beacon with its top
section painted red
and complete with a
small white lantern.

In the early nineteenth century, the eastern tip of Anglesey was a graveyard both for ships entering the Menai Strait from the north and for those in Red Wharf Bay awaiting fair weather before rounding the Skerries. On 17 August 1831 an incident took place which in all probability hastened the decision to provide an aid to navigation in this dangerous area.

The steamer Rothsay Castle, on her regular trip from Liverpool to the Menai Straits, left Liverpool at about 11am but because of the rough weather she made little headway. Despite requests from the passengers the captain refused to turn back. By midnight he had still not made land and an hour later she struck Dutchman Bank and, out of control, struck a sandbank off Penmon. Of the 150 passengers on board, 130 were lost.

As a result, Trinity House agreed to erect a lighthouse on a reef off the mainland between Trwyn Du or Black Head and Puffin Island. Commenced in 1837, it was a 96ft circular black and white stone tower stepped at the base with a single step halfway. Completed by James Walker at a cost of £11,589, the acetylene-powered light was first exhibited in 1838. The castellated gallery is painted black with the white lantern showing a flashing white light visible for twelve miles, topped by a conical roof complete with a weather vane.

The lighthouse, although not particularly spectacular, is noteworthy as the first wave washed lighthouse built by James Walker, and is thus the forerunner of his more famous lights at The Needles, Smalls and Wolf Rock. Some of the innovative features included a stepped base with vertical walls, as distinct from the graceful curves normally incorporated into such towers.

The lighthouse, sometimes known as Penmon or Black Rock, was originally manned by two keepers but it was converted to automated acetylene in 1922 and the keepers were withdrawn. It was converted to solar power in 1996 when a Tideland 1300 lantern with a first order catadioptric fixed lens and a thirty-five-Watt halogen lamp were installed with a range of twelve miles. Another feature of the renovations of 1996 was a unique mechanism to sound the fog signal, which comprises a 178 kilogram bell which is struck once every sixty seconds.

Although the lighthouse marks the reef offshore, the straight between Puffin Island and the mainland has a rocky outcrop called Perch Rock in the middle of the channel. This rock, a short distance to the east of the light, is marked by a beacon.

Great Orme

The lighthouse on Great Orme at Llandudno is perhaps noteworthy more for its internal than external appearance. Constructed in 1862 for the Mersey Docks and Harbour Company to the design of engineer-in-chief George Lister, who also worked on alterations to the Point Lynas light in 1871, it was cut into steep limestone cliffs on the most northerly point of Great Orme's Head, 325ft above sea level, to became the highest lighthouse in Wales.

The need for a lighthouse on the Great Orme was first recognised in 1861, and a letter recommending its establishment was approved by Trinity House. Constructed with dressed limestone, the building's 37ft high walls were topped with castellated edges and the two-storey accommodation had a flat roof. The light was displayed from a semi-circular lamp room attached to the seaward side of the building at ground level, similar to Point Lynas. An interesting internal feature was the extensive use of Canadian pine boarding inside the accommodation block which,

at 20ft high, provided privacy between the main keeper's and second keeper's accommodation.

The flashing white light, visible for twenty-four miles and first shown on 1 December 1862, was created by paraffin wick burners. These were replaced in 1904 by vaporising petroleum mantle-burners, which were in turn superseded in 1923 by dissolved acetylene mantle-lamps. The station, electrified in 1965, passed into Trinity House's control in 1973 and a white rendering was applied. The light was extinguished on 22 March 1985 and control of the building reverted to the Mersey Docks and Harbour Company, which subsequently sold the property.

The Fresnel lens is now an exhibit at the Orme's Summit Visitor Centre, where it can be seen illuminated to give an idea of its intensity. Situated in the Great Orme Country Park, the lighthouse is now a bed and breakfast in which the old lamp room is used as the sitting room offering sea views. The bedrooms are named after the use the rooms were put to during the light's operational era.

▶▶ Despite its squat appearance, the Great Orme light was the highest in Wales.

▶ The plaque surmounting the central doorway on the south-eastern side records the building's origins.

Point of Ayr

In medieval times Chester was an important port dealing mainly with the French wine exporting region and Liverpool was still a small creek. The entry into the Dee was treacherous, so as early as the thirteenth century lights were displayed at Whitford Garn in Flintshire and Hilbre Island off Hoylake, for which the Earl of Chester paid an annual sum for thier upkeep. Although the Dee was canalised in 1733 to enable larger ships to navigate it, it was not until 1776, following the loss of the Dublin packets Nonpariel and Trevor, that proposals to improve the lighting arrangements were carried out.

Initially it was suggested that two lighthouses and a series of buoys be provided, but the cost was prohibitive. A wooden lighthouse built on the surrounding hillside was suggested, but it was eventually agreed that a lighthouse should built at Point of Ayr. Situated at Talacre to the east of Prestatyn, on the northernmost point of the west side of the Dee estuary, this lighthouse was one of a series which guarded Liverpool Bay.

Today, due to the change in the coastline, it is difficult to appreciate how lights at Hoylake, Bidston Hill and Leasowe interacted with Point of Ayr or Y Parlwr Du, Talacre. Locally it was known as the lake light to distinguish it from the two lights at Leasowe, which were referred to as the sea lights.

Designed by H. Turner, it was built at a cost of £349 8s 1d and the 52ft circular stone tower, complete with gallery and lantern, was supported on screw piles driven into the sand. The tower had three floors with a basement coal store. The lighthouse now lies between the high and low watermarks.

In 1819 Trinity House took over responsibility for the lighthouse and in 1820 had it refurbished, increasing the height to 58ft and installing a new lantern which exists today and is reputedly the oldest in Wales.

When operational the tower was painted in alternate red and white bands, with a red gallery and a white lantern with a red roof. One white light shining seaward towards Llandudno was displayed from the lantern, with a second facing down the Dee towards Dawpool in Cheshire at a height of 8ft. The lights were discontinued in 1844 when a new screw pile lighthouse designed by James Walker was built by Gordon & Co of Deptford.

This structure was made up of nine cast iron piles driven into the sand with one central and eight outer supports. There was a double-skinned corrugated iron accommodation block, on top of which was a gunmetal lantern. In 1883 this light was replaced by a lightship and nothing remains of the pile light.

The lighthouse is now well below the high tide mark and is only isolated at low tide. In 1996 the tower was restored and it is currently all white with a black gallery and a red lantern. The original small attached dwelling has been demolished.

►► The lighthouse at Point of Ayr, at the entrance to the river Dee, is now a historic attraction managed by Flintshire County Council.

Glossary

Acetylene A highly combustible gas which burns with an intensely bright flame.

Argand lamp A bright and relatively clean-burning lamp invented by Francois-Pierre Ami Argand in 1783.

Automated An unmanned light controlled externally; all the major UK lighthouses are automated, with Trinity House controlling and monitoring its lights from the Corporation's Depot in Harwich.

Beacon A structure, usually land based, either lit or unlit, used to guide mariners.

Characteristic The identifying feature of a lighthouse is its characteristic; for example, the light could be described as fixed, or flashing.

Daymark Light towers often also serve as daymarks, landmarks that are visible from the sea during daylight acting as aids to navigation.

Dioptric lens A development by Augustin Fresnel consisting of a bull's eye lens surrounded by a series of concentric glass prisms. Dioptric lenses were classified by the focal length.

Elevation The elevation refers to a light's height above sea level; the higher the elevation, the greater the range.

Flashing light A light where the period of light is less than the period of darkness.

Fog signals A sound signal used to warn mariners in times of fog or heavy weather.

Gallery A walkway beneath the lantern room to enable access for maintenance.

Group flashing A series of flashing lights followed by a period of darkness.

High light The taller or higher of a pair of lights.

Isophase light A light characteristic where the periods of light and dark shown are equal.

Keepers The persons responsible for maintaining and keeping the light at an aid to navigation, including the associated buildings.

Lanby The abbreviated term for Large Automatic Navigation Buoy, a modern floating unmanned aid to navigation often used in place of a lightship.

Lanterns The glass-enclosed space at the top of a lighthouse housing the lens or optic; lanterns are often encircled by a narrow walkway called the gallery.

Lightship A vessel, powered or unpowered, designed to support a navigational aid.

Low light The shorter or lower of the two lights used to mark a channel or hazard.

Occulting A way of making a light appear to flash by blocking the light with an opaque panel.

Range lights Lights displayed in pairs which mark a navigable channel.

Reflector A system which intensifies light by reflecting the light source into a beam, both to increase intensity and to enable the beam to be manipulated to produce differing light characteristics.

Bibliography

Bowen, J. P.: British Lighthouses (Longmans, London, 1947).

Hague, Douglas B.: Lighthouses of Wales: their architecture and archaeology (Royal Commission on the Ancient and Historical Monuments of Wales, 1994).

Hague, Douglas B. and Christie, Rosemary: Lighthouses: Their Architecture, History and Archaeology (Gomer Press, Dyfed, 1975).

Jackson, Derrick: Lighthouses of England and Wales (David & Charles, Devon, 1975).

Nicholson, Christopher: Rock Lighthouses of Britain (Patrick Stephens, Somerset, 1995).

Sutton-Jones, Kenneth: To Safely Guide Their Way: Lighthouses and Maritime Aids of the World (B&T Publications, Southampton, 1998).

Woodman, Richard and Wilson, Jane: The Lighthouses of Trinity House (Thomas Reed Publications, 2002).

Websites

www.lighthousedepot.com
Comprehensive list of world lights with details, photos, locations and links.

www.trabas.de/enindex.html
List of world lights including minor lights with photos.

www.unc.edu/~rowlett/lighthouse/index.htm
Comprehensive list of world lights with historic outline, photographs and links.

www.trinityhouse.co.uk
Trinity House website with details of all their lighthouses.

www.michaelmillichamp.ukgateway.net Main focus is on England and Wales with details of operational and non-operational lights.

www.lighthousesrus.org
Mainly an American lighthouse site, it has photos and details of British lights.

Acknowledgements

A number of people have assisted with the compilation of this book. The following helped in various ways and we are grateful to Vikki Gilson at Trinity House; Geoff Badland at Strumble Head; Brian Thomson of the Holyhead lifeboat; Dave Herbert of Portishead Lifeboat; Gareth Williams and his Stena Line colleagues at Fishguard port; Porthcawl lifeboat station; and Alf Pritchard. The work of the late Douglas Hague has been utilised and his contribution to the history of Welsh lighthouses is acknowledged.

All photographs are by Nicholas Leach, except the following: Tony Denton pages 12, 13, 14, 15, 44; Trinity House 49, 51, 53, 57, 66; supplied by Michel Forand 7, 8; Gerry Douglas-Sherwood, Archivist, Association of Lighthouse Keepers 36, 46, 66; Mat Dickson 50, 54, 56; Porthcawl lifeboat station 30; and Alf Pritchard 72.

Index